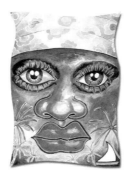

Published in 2002 by
The Gallery Publications
P.O. Box 3181 Zanzibar
email: gallery@swahilicoast.com

© The Gallery Publications
By Pascal Bogaert
Edited by Gemma Pitcher

ISBN 9987 667 11 2

the KRAZY book of KANGAS

Pascal Bogaert

Published by The Gallery Publications

INTRODUCTION

What is a Kanga?

A kanga is simply a piece of brightly coloured and patterned cotton cloth with a proverb written in Swahili across it. Kanga are sold as pairs, starched, folded and encased in plastic wrappings, in every tiny, hot and sweaty little shop in every big, hot and sweaty market in all the vast, hot and sweaty regions of East Africa. They are worn as skirts and headscarves by ladies of all religions, colours, shapes and sizes, mostly because they are cheap, cool and easy to wash, but also because the proverbs written on them are perfect for communicating messages better left unsaid.

They say a picture paints a thousand words; but a kanga can start or end a marriage, begin a village feud lasting several generations or win a general election. It's the proverbs on the kanga that are the important part, you see – a straying husband, for example, tiptoeing home and peeking around his kitchen door, need only catch a glimpse of his wife's reproachful behind, emblazoned with the words "Why Go Shopping for Food When You Have Meat at Home?" to know he's in BIG trouble...

Kanga History

Kangas were originally brought to the shores of East Africa by the Portuguese. Actually they're probably the only good idea the Portuguese came up with here – their other imports were mostly things like bull-fighting, syphilis and various new and horrible ways to kill people (they also introduced the word for 'masturbation' into the Swahili vocabulary, but that's another story). Portuguese squares of cloth, called 'leso' were eventually converted into the long, rectangular double kanga shapes we see today, and the name 'kanga' was born. Kanga is the Swahili word for guinea fowl – a brightly coloured, noisy, chattering and vain bird that likes to go around in large groups. Scholars say the word for guinea fowl was used because the original cloth pattern was dark with white spots like the guinea fowl's plumage, but the word was actually coined by a pissed-off African husband after a particularly raucous party with his wives, aunts and sisters...

Once it took off, the kanga went from strength to strength and quickly became the garment of choice for the ladies of Tanzania, Kenya and Uganda. Naturally, its manufacture was immediately moved to the sweat shops of India, East Asia and China, with the kangas being re-imported into East Africa at ridiculously cheap prices.

Kanga today

The elegant, frivolous drapes of cloth that adorn the bodies of pretty, vivacious African girls soon caught the eye of dumpy, dreary exchange students and Peace Corps volunteers, who started ineptly wrapping them around their frumpy waists and wearing them with clompy sandals at college parties to demonstrate how ethnic and globally aware they were. This created a brisk export market, with canny African entrepreneurs shipping kangas over to the western world and selling them to fools like these at $20 a pop.

But back here is still Africa – one cigarette, twenty people – and so the kanga has taken on a million new uses, from the mundane to the ingenious. A kanga may begin its life stretched crisply and alluringly across a smart lady's backside – but it will end up as a sad scrap of encrusted rag, tucked into the overalls of a dalla-dalla mechanic or wiping up vomit from a sick baby.

Our little book presents a few uses of the kanga we can guarantee no-one has ever thought of (mainly because there aren't many people out there as sick as us), together with a few more practical hints about how to tie that souvenir you've just bought. Enjoy!

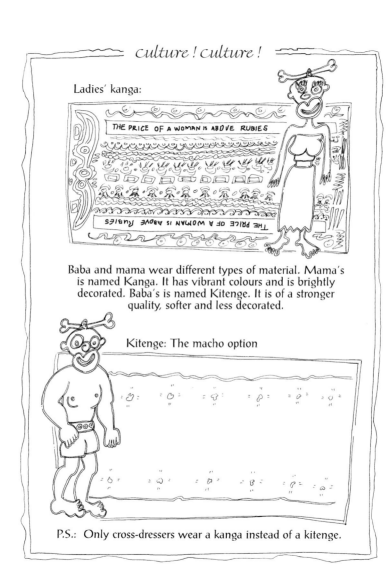

Ladies' kanga:

THE PRICE OF A WOMAN IS ABOVE RUBIES

Baba and mama wear different types of material. Mama's is named Kanga. It has vibrant colours and is brightly decorated. Baba's is named Kitenge. It is of a stronger quality, softer and less decorated.

Kitenge: The macho option

P.S.: Only cross-dressers wear a kanga instead of a kitenge.

Baby on the back style

African social
security ....

Kanga shop as seen in Zanzibar

Front loading baby carrier

For left handed
babies

For right
handed babies

cape style

IS IT A BIRD? IS IT A PLANE?

IS IT A BIRD? IS IT A PLANE?

Super (kanga)
woman!!!

Party style

shawl style

Drape it over the shoulders

Left and right

Tuck it in at the neck

knot in
front

Cigarette Style – presented to you by Fatima

Just roll the kanga around your body as when you prepare a cigarette.

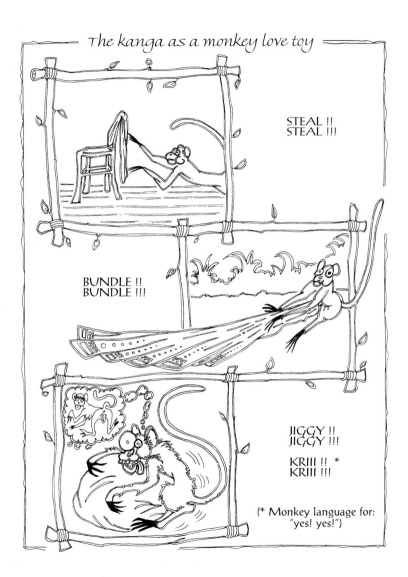

To hide your Elephantitis after returning to your office from your safari

It will help you get accepted faster by your colleagues at work !!

Feeling Demure ?

Drape your kanga over the shoulders and knot in front for a modest look.....

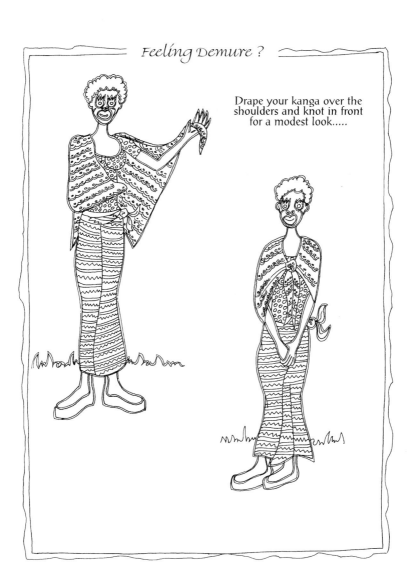

How a kanga will bring you fame and fortune!

*More daring girls wear
their kangas like this*

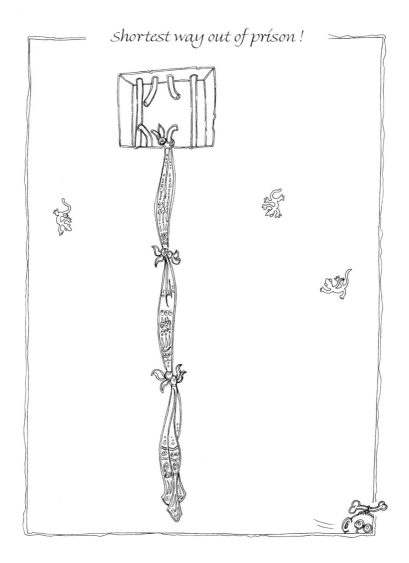

shortest way out of prison !

The traditional muslim women of Zanzibar wear their kangas like this.

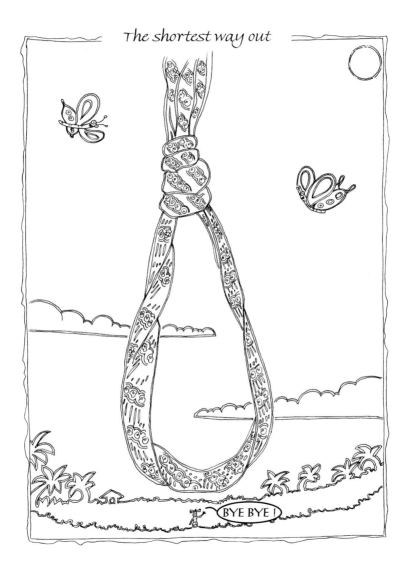

Hood style

Knot in front

They say that the Dalai Lama can no longer find his Karma without his kanga

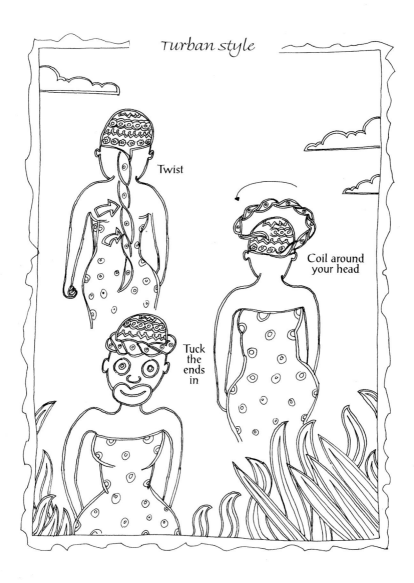

Turban style

Twist

Coil around
your head

Tuck
the
ends
in

A horror riddle: find the African ghost

combined headscarf and shawl

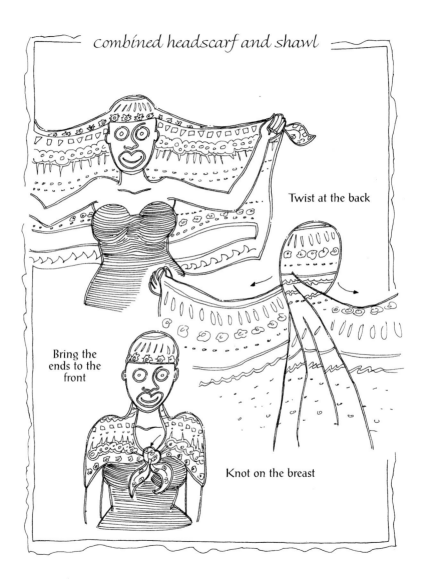

Twist at the back

Bring the ends to the front

Knot on the breast

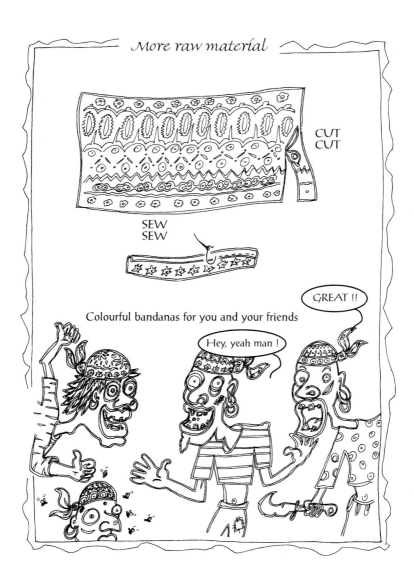

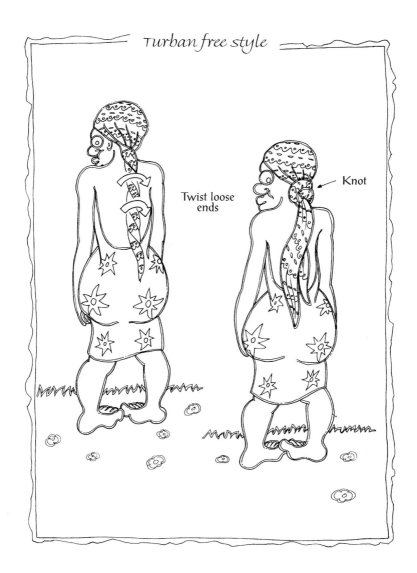

Turban free style

Twist loose ends

Knot

Fold

Keep your lunch safe on safari

Mini skirt

Fold together

IF YOU'VE GOT IT, FLAUNT IT!

Knot at the side

FLAUNT IT!

Fold in half lengthways

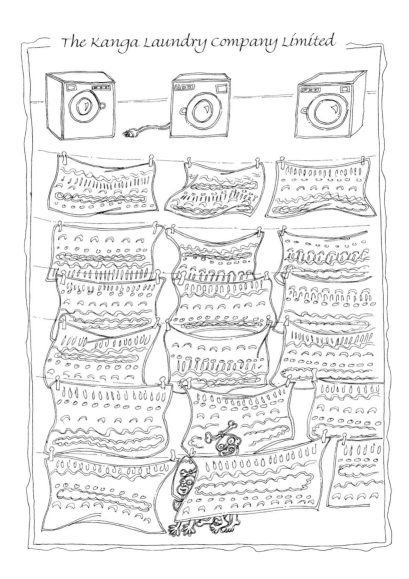

(Not to be worn in public places, behind closed doors only)

(Not to be practised in public places ....)

Ero style – double

(Strictly for private viewing)

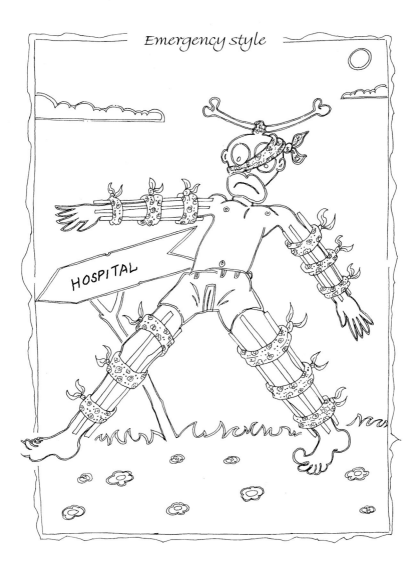

Emergency style

Love goes with a present in Africa !

Kanga: even useful for the famous
'**three legged**' man of Zanzibar

Bikini style II

Knot in front

Bring ends to the front and knot

Bring the other ends to the back and knot

Boob Tube

Knot at the back

Bush bikini style

swimsuit (G-string style)

Knot in the front above the bosom

Pass between legs

Knot at the back

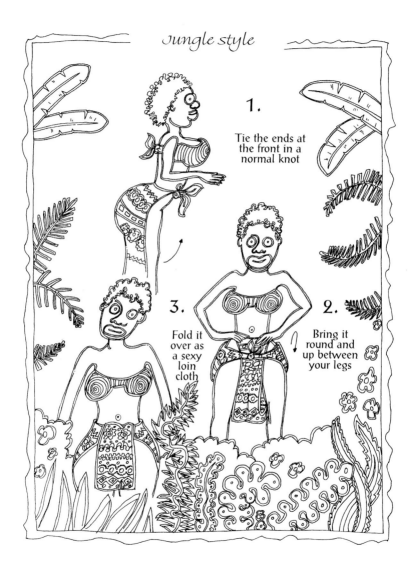

Kanga tip

A knot in the upper corner of your kanga will prevent it slipping off

DON'T GET CAUGHT WITH YOUR PANTS DOWN

DON'T GET CAUGHT WITH YOUR PANTS DOWN

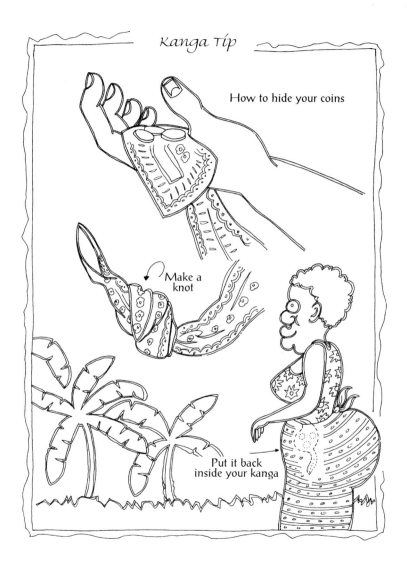

They make great cushion covers

washing!

99% of all African kangas are still washed by hand and dried in the hot sun afterwards

As a pad for heavy loads

As decoration

Used in many hotels and restaurants
along the East African coast

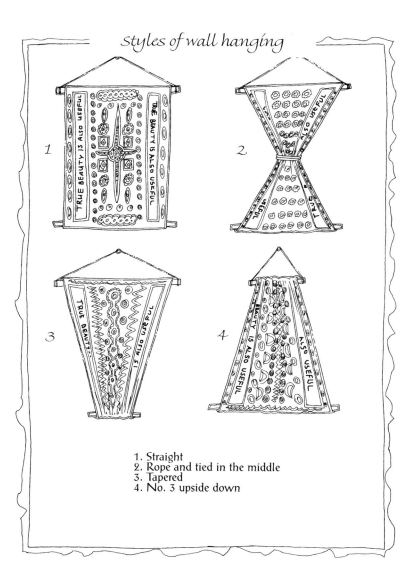

styles of wall hanging

1. Straight
2. Rope and tied in the middle
3. Tapered
4. No. 3 upside down

Women use their kangas to catch a small
type of fish named 'dagaa'

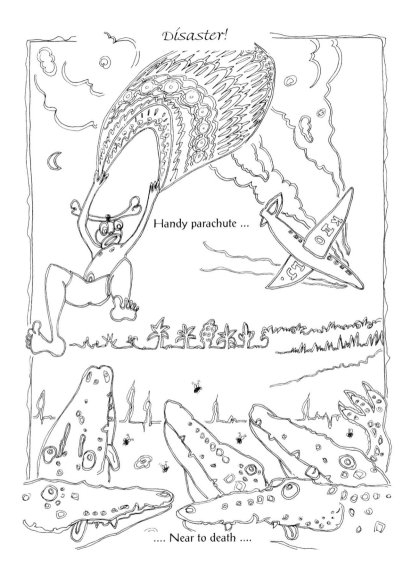

... But there's always a solution in Africa !

Mbolo used his kanga well !

Draw your own kanga style:

Draw your own kanga style:

Draw your own kanga style:

Draw your own kanga style:

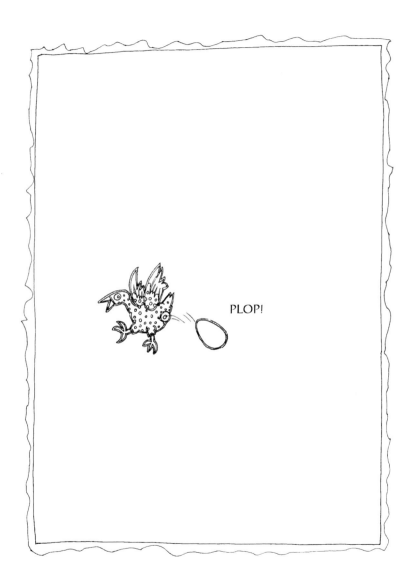

PLOP!

CRACK!!